REMEMBRANCES: JOURNEY OF A THERAPEUTIC MUSICIAN

Remembrances: Journey of a Therapeutic Musician

Donese Mayfield

ISBN: 1539393844
ISBN 13: 9781539393849
Library of Congress Control Number: 2016916891
CreateSpace Independent Publishing Platform
North Charleston, South Carolina

Cover photo credits: Omar Durant

TABLE OF CONTENTS

INTRODUCTION

I have a story to tell. It has to do with birth, death, life transitions in between and with music that calms and soothes people going through these transitions. We go through many transitions in our lives beginning with birth and ending with death. I want to share my place in all of this as a musician, where I came from, how I got here, what I have learned along the way and what I do with this unusual work as a therapeutic musician.

Much of what I have to tell you is in the form of stories, stories about hospice patients I have played for, stories about a wide variety of transitional experiences I have witnessed and stories about bereaved families comforted by music. Therapeutic music can be entertainment, comfort, medicine and prayer. It can create joy and pleasure, ease suffering and facilitate change. The instrument I use in this work is a small, twenty-six string Celtic harp. It is my workhorse. It can play a wide variety of music from country western to The Beatles, golden oldies to classical tunes, lullabies and hymns. Music can match a patient's breathing and comfort and soothe grieving families.

End-stage patients may suffer chronic anxiety or pain, terminal restlessness or agitation. A therapeutic musician can assist the patient by helping them achieve a balanced internal state, a steady state or homeostasis. A musician may use arrhythmic music, atonal music or familiar music attuned to the patient's cultural or religious background or emotional state. Often, profound changes in the patient's state will occur within 15 to 30 minutes. Changes include going to sleep, relaxation of facial muscles, changes in color, more regular breathing, changes in blood pressure and changes in heart rate.

Here is one of many interesting stories I experienced along this journey, one that has greatly affected me and how I approach patients. This story has to do with birth, the transition we all make into this life.

THE BIRTH OF DONALD

K athleen is a hospice nurse. She's been present in the room when I play my harp for those who are dying. We have worked together on some challenging, complex hospice situations. Now, she was about to give birth. "Would you play the harp at this birthing?" she asked, inviting me into her sacred space. The last time I was in labor and delivery was when my son was born 42 years ago. Yet, on a cold night in January, I met Kathleen, her husband and her mid-wife at the hospital.

A fetal monitor on Kathleen's belly let us all hear and see the baby's heart rhythm. I matched the music I played to that rhythm. Then, when Kathleen would feel a contraction and begin to breathe through it, I would switch the music to match her new breathing pattern. This process is called *entrainment* (more about this later). The short, quick breaths coming from her were matched by short, quick rhythms on the strings. I played lullabies as her breathing slowed, sweet music to ease both the mother and the baby. Kathleen's breathing patterns changed and her pain and anxiety eased. Suddenly, the baby's head had crowned and his body flowed gently into the world. There was no crying and he was a healthy, beautiful, content and mellow little baby. He was named Donald. He heard the harp music before he made his entrance into this world. He will always love the sound of harp music! Today Donald is a normal, 13-year old boy who plays sports and just happens to like music!

Chapter 1

In the Beginning

Music - a universal language.
Play, listen, be present.

Just about everything in the past seventy years of my life has been in preparation for this work, though I have only recently come to realize it. I came from a medical family. My dad was a small-town doctor who practiced what is now considered very old-fashioned medicine. He made house calls, even in the middle of the night, if someone was really sick. His patients knew our home phone number. My mother had nurse's training. She ran the office and handled the billing. If patients couldn't afford to pay, then arrangements were made. But they received medical care for their illness regardless of financial circumstances. At Christmas, we were brought all sorts of food and gifts. Sometimes I'd wait in the car behind the hospital when Dad made his hospital rounds. Once I watched behind a glass enclosure in the operating room while Dad performed surgery. Medicine was an integral part of our family.

I've played music all my life and studied piano from age six through my high school years. I also studied the organ for two years and have been a church organist in years past. Yet, there have been times in my busy life that music had no place and there were times that music had a much different place than today.

I have always been an educator, teaching business subjects in high school and vocational school and teaching CPR and First Aid for the Red Cross. At Sandia National Laboratory in Albuquerque, I designed curriculum and training classes for Air Force technicians and the Security Force. As a government contractor, I designed and taught classes for technical managers. Educating has always been a very important part of my life.

I discovered the harp at age forty-two and found my passion. I fell in love with the instrument. I had played music all of my life, but I suddenly discovered that with the harp, I didn't just play music, I was a musician! What fun! I could play tunes and this discovery started me on the journey to therapeutic music work. I now educate people about dying, sometimes with a few words, but mostly with healing sounds from the harp. When I say healing, I am referring to emotional and spiritual healing. This is a completely different concept from curing. Curing is symptom-driven and focuses on fixing something that is wrong with the body. It is physiological in nature. Healing means coming to an acceptance of and peace with oneself and one's life. Healing is holistic and integrates spirit, heart, mind and body. There can be healing in dying, contrary to the view in Western medicine that sees death as failure. There can also be healing in a family as they gather.

Who I Am Today

When people ask what I do, I tell them I am a musician. I play the Celtic harp, the piano and the organ. Most of my work now is therapeutic music working with hospice patients. This statement about my work oftentimes creates a pause, an awkward silence or evokes some rather interesting responses from people such as:

*   Oh, I could never do that work. It's too depressing.
*   How can you do that kind of work? It must be terribly hard.
*   God bless you. You have a real ministry/calling.

Sometimes, I say nothing because people just don't want to go there. It's too scary. Other times, I respond to this by saying that the work is not at all depressing. When I, as part of an interdisciplinary hospice team, can help create a graceful passage for a hospice patient, it can be a really beautiful experience, a sacred moment, a good death, a blessed passing.

There is no greater gift to receive than to be present at such a spiritual event. It is a privilege and an honor. I have come to realize over the years that it is a real calling for me.

Sometimes, when people learn about my work, they respond by sharing their personal experiences of family members' deaths. One beautiful story told to me by a woman was about her brother. He had been a principal dancer with a nationally famous dance troupe in the early 1980's. And, by the late 1980's he was dying of AIDS. His body was ravaged and the right side of his brain was full of lesions. His death was only hours, maybe even minutes away. His sister said to me, "I was playing his favorite music, Mahler's *Song of the Earth*, with my hand lightly placed on his chest. As the song's last note played, he took his last breath and crossed over."

Many of the hospice patients I am with at the end of their lives are actively dying. This is a clinical term used to describe a person's last few hours of life as the body shuts down. The music I play at the bed-side with an actively dying patient is much different from what most people think of as music. Therapeutic music matches the breathing pattern of the patient in the moment and follows the concept of *entrainment* or *bio-musicology*. Entrainment is the synchronization of an organism to an external rhythm.[i] It is a concept that is used in physics, engineering and hydrodynamics, just to mention a few disciplines. Van Morrison wrote a song entitled, *That's Entrainment*, which was included in his 2008 album, *Keep It Simple*. Morrison described the meaning of the word entrainment and the music on the album as follows, "Entrainment is when you connect with the music. Entrainment is really what I'm getting at in the music. It's kind of when you're in the present moment, you're here, with no past or future."[ii] For a very quick, easy-to-understand example, notice how you pat your foot or drum your fingers rhythmically when you hear certain types of music. That's an example of entrainment.[iii]

I rhythmically entrain with the breathing of a patient by matching their breathing pattern. In the final hours of life, as people transition, there are a variety of breathing patterns and I observe and physically breathe with the patient for a short while to get a sense of their rhythm and then I play that rhythm. About 80-90% of the time, the breathing rhythm of the patient will slow down, relax and settle. This change occurs within 10-30 minutes. I cannot explain it. Yet, I tell patients' families that we should all have someone playing a harp at our bed-side. What a way to go!

THE DEAF CAN HEAR

Hearing is the last sense to go. It is the first sense to begin developing in the womb at around six weeks and it is the last sense to go in this life. It does not matter if a patient is comatose, deaf, medicated or doesn't have his/her hearing aids in. The patient hears. Live music changes the energy in the air. It changes the way the air oscillates around the patient and they hear, even at a cellular level through their skin, through their bodies. They somehow sense the sound vibrations in the air. Remember this as you read these stories.

Another experience that demonstrates the power of music involved Robert, an instructor at the Santa Fe School for the Deaf. I had visited Robert previously, but this time, as I went into his room, two of his former students were visiting him. I introduced myself and briefly explained my work. Both hearing-impaired students communicated with sign language and one of them could read my lips and had some language capability. After much signing between the students, the student with language ability asked if the other student could put his hands on my harp. I readily agreed, not knowing what would happen. The student placed both hands on the sound board as I began to play. A few minutes later, as I watched him, tears started streaming down his cheeks. He was hearing the music in his own way and it touched him in some way that I, as a hearing person, could not imagine. We sat there for quite some time as I played the harp and, he, with his hands on the harp, listened. The power of music!

MUSIC THERAPY VS. THERAPEUTIC MUSIC

Before we venture any further, let's explore the difference between music therapy and therapeutic music. Music therapy uses music as a tool for development and is a goal-oriented therapy. Think of music therapy in the same context as physical therapy or occupational therapy or art therapy. The therapist is working interactively with the patient toward a specific goal by using a variety of means to accomplish that goal. In the case of music therapy, the therapist is working toward a non-musical goal and is using music as the medium by which to accomplish that goal. "Music therapy is the prescribed use of music by a qualified person to effect positive changes in the psychological, physical, cognitive or social functioning of individuals with health or educational problems."[iv]

I am a certified therapeutic musician. A therapeutic musician uses music as a healing modality and has no expectations or judgments about the situation. The work is service, not performance, oriented. This means that my focus is completely on the patient and I react to the situation in real time. In other words, I work totally in the moment with whatever the circumstances happen to be - for example, family dynamics, a patient's terminal anxiety or pain issues or young children at the bed-side. I have no agenda. There is no intention. The work is open-ended and completely in the moment.

As a therapeutic musician, I frequently play for small groups of elders in assisted living facilities. When I play for these groups, I include songs such as *Stardust, Over the Rainbow* and *I'm in the Mood for Love.* These songs take many of us back to a time in our lives when we were younger, maybe in love or maybe ballroom dancing. Memories of certain songs and music are different for each of us at different times and places in our lives, another illustration of the power of music.

I frequently play for groups with more impaired cognitive levels. These elders have a wide variety of dementia and Alzheimer's symptoms. Oftentimes, in the advanced stages of these diseases, patients lose their ability to speak. However, music is stored in a different part of the brain than speech.

And when I begin to sing songs such as *You Are My Sunshine*, *My Bonnie Lies over the Ocean* and songs they knew in their younger years, these non-verbal patients oftentimes start to sing! At first I was amazed. It happened so often that I researched and found that this happens frequently with non-verbal patients - once again, the power of music![v]

STELLA, WALTZING IN THE MOMENT

Here is a beautiful story of the value of therapeutic music. As I played my harp for Stella in her final hours, she breathed a perfect 3/4 rhythm, that's a waltz rhythm like the *Tennessee Waltz* or *Edelweiss*. No deviation, no variation, a perfect waltz time. As I entrained with her, Stella was having no part of it. She was doing her thing. I finally asked Stella's daughter if, by chance, Stella had been a dancer. I played the *Tennessee Waltz* to show her daughter what was happening as Stella "danced" with her breath. With no hesitation, her daughter said, "Mom and Dad were wonderful ballroom dancers." Her dad had died many years ago. "I think your Mom and Dad are off waltzing together somewhere right now," I said. We sat there together in a cathartic moment and reflected on that image. Stella passed shortly after that. Her daughter was left with a beautiful image and memory of her Mother and Dad dancing. A year later, when Stella's daughter saw our hospice nurse, she still remembered that beautiful image and recounted that experience.

In The Moment with Vivian

Vivian had a reputation for hitting and biting anyone who tried to work with her, which included anyone trying to bathe, dress or feed her. She was well known in the nursing facility. Knowing this, I approached her from a distance and offered her music. Needless to say, I stayed outside of hitting range. She was okay with the idea, and so I sat in a small chair next to her, but not too close, and played tunes and more tunes. She enjoyed the music and began to respond to it. She really became quite pleasant as I continued with a variety of music. With that reaction, I played even more. By the time I was ready to leave, Vivian held my hand and told me she loved me. Ah, the power of music!

Chapter 2

A CLOSER LOOK AT WHAT HAPPENS

Transitions we make
Into and out of this life -
Joy, grief, much else.

We transition into this life by way of the birth process and we transition out of this life by way of the death process. And there are many similarities between these two transitional processes as mentioned in the earlier story of Donald's birth.

"All transitions have similar key elements. As well, every person experiences a wide variety of transitions during the course of his/her lifetime. In that sense, there is nothing new in the dying process. In fact, each of us develops our own, personal style for dealing with transitions. We tend to stick with that style, whatever it might be, when we face the transition we call death. If you would like to know how you will handle your own death, look back upon your life and observe how you have handled all your other transitions. Unless you decide to change your approach, that is how you will die.

While all transitions have similar key elements, every person does not experience every sign or symptom. A person may experience a particular sign or symptom in his or her own unique way. There is room for infinite variation in how any given individual may experience the dying process. At the same time, certain general themes are common to all. It is well to remember that all transitions entail some disagreeable or uncomfortable aspects and the process of dying is no exception. No reasonable person expects that life will contain no discomforts, yet some espouse the notion that somehow, death will. This is not a reasonable expectation. The dying process may have its difficult aspects regardless of one's level of enlightenment. Modern medicine has demonstrated a remarkable capacity for mitigating or even eliminating many disagreeable aspects of physical death. At the same time, modern medicine cannot relieve people of responsibility for their own lives. We all prepare for our own death by the manner in which we live our lives. Skilled clinicians can be a great help, but we each bear the ultimate burden of responsibility for how we live and how we die."[vi]

CHARLES' STORY

"Charles lived a crappy life and he's dying a crappy death," said David, the hospice nurse, when he called me. "See what you can do to help. I've given him all the pain medication I can." As I entered his room in the nursing home, Charles was fighting his demons, thrashing, hallucinating and writhing. I sat away from his bed-side, though I knew he was actively dying. The entire scene was very troubling, even a bit scary. The chaplain tried to hold Charles' hand and speak softly to no avail. I began to play my small harp with no expectations and some fear and concern. Though I knew he was actively dying, I had some concern that he could jump out of that bed and go charging around! He was so very agitated. To my surprise and the chaplain's, Charles calmed down and was asleep within twenty minutes. I played for a couple of hours until I grew tired. Charles died an hour later. The chaplain used the word miracle to describe Charles' calming. I am not comfortable with that word. However, Charles was healed at some emotional or spiritual level and was able to move on, that I affirm.

Unfinished Business

Early in this work, several experiences made me realize the power and cathartic effect of music once again. As I played music for a gentleman named Joe, I sensed that he wanted to say something. He even seemed driven to speak to me about something that weighed on him. Finally, as I took a break in the music, Joe looked at me and said, "My family thinks I abused my children, but I didn't." WOW! How do you respond to a statement like that? I murmured sympathetically. This was obviously some kind of statement he needed to make. Or maybe he just needed to set the record straight, I wasn't sure. But as I left his room, I called our hospice social worker to turn this information over to her. I had no idea what to do with it. This experience got totally eclipsed when another patient confided that he had killed someone. GOOD GRIEF! What am I supposed to do with this information? How do I respond? Is the patient hallucinating? This time I called the social worker and the chaplain.

Unfinished business is a term that will be discussed in more depth as we move through many hospice stories. It is a term that refers to life experiences that are emotionally unfinished or incomplete, experiences that are in need of emotional and spiritual resolution. Completing what is unfinished leads to emotional healing and, ideally, spiritual growth, and effects spirit, mind and body. Sometimes, family members may be estranged from one another or possibly from the hospice patient. A patient can sense this energetic tension and may decide to hold on, so to speak, until emotional issues are resolved.

MARY AND COMPLETING UNFINISHED BUSINESS

This is a story about Mary and the remarkable experience I shared with her as she chose to complete unfinished business before passing over. Mary was in a coma in the Intensive Care Unit (ICU) and not expected to live through the night. I received a call via the church prayer chain to pray for her. "And by the way," the caller said to me, "Mary's daughter is a professional harpist in Minneapolis." "Oh," I said, "please tell her I'd be happy to lend her my harp if she'd like to play for her mother." Twenty minutes later my phone rang. Mary's daughter asked me to play for her mother.

The power of music, therapeutic music, healing properties of music, all terms I had heard of and read about but never experienced, were about to teach me lessons of life and death over the next few weeks. I hauled my harp to the ICU with no idea of what to expect or what lay ahead of me over the next hours.

As I played for Mary, I figured out the monitors and could see her breathing and heart rate change and settle. WOW! The power of live music! Mary came out of her coma and lived another month. I have learned to call these amazing experiences *unfinished business*. Her son and daughter came several times and worked out their unfinished business. As mentioned earlier, completing unfinished business is about emotional healing and centers on relationships, and, ideally, spiritual growth. I played for Mary several times during that one month period. I played tunes like *Danny Boy*, *Greensleeves* and *Silent Night*. Once I started playing *Amazing Grace* and oops, Mary's facial expression dramatically changed. I don't know where I had taken her, but it scared me. I quickly changed the music. Once again, I learned the power of music and how to enter through the back door.

Mary died a month later while I was on a business trip to Oak Ridge. It wasn't supposed to happen that way. My agenda didn't include her dying like that while I was gone and when I thought she was doing okay. Finding her phone number in the directory, I called it on the outside chance that a family member would answer. Her daughter did. "What happened?" I asked in an effort to make sense of the unexplainable. "Mary was awake and aware when I left her a few days ago." In a hushed, reverent tone, Mary's daughter made sense of it for me. Mary finished her business with her family. She then called her family and medical team to her bed-side and requested them to disconnect the tubes. She was made to repeat the request several times. Her request was honored.

Often, we see a process whereby family members come to say goodbye to the dying person. This can be a way of giving the person permission to move on. Frequently, when family members cannot travel to see the patient, hospice staff will hold a cell phone up to the patient's ear to allow the patient to hear family members telling them goodbye. Remember, hearing is the last sense to go. Oftentimes when a patient knows a family member is coming in, the patient will 'hold on' until the family member arrives. Patients have also been known to 'hold on' for birthdays, anniversaries and special holidays.

WILLIE'S FAMILY

I'd like to share another example of how the power of music created an atmosphere of healing for a family at their dying father's bed-side. I had played for Willie a few days earlier when his daughter was there. She was his primary caregiver. When I went to see him the second time, Willie's son and daughter-in-law were also there. There seemed to be some family tension which is not uncommon at a dying parent's bed-side.

After introducing myself and being given permission to play music, I sat in the back of the room and quietly began to play. Very soon, I noticed the son start to cry. Then his wife also began to cry. Nothing had been said among the family members. Shortly after that, the son, his wife, and his sister all moved to the bed-side together. Then they held hands. After standing like that for a while, they began to pray. I continued to play quietly. Whatever created the tension, who knows? But some kind of spiritual and emotional healing took place. Once again, the power of music!

SPIRITUAL GROWTH AT THE END STAGE OF LIFE

Here is a beautiful story about spiritual growth at the end of life excerpted from a sermon by Laurence T. Cotter. A few weeks ago, a hospice patient asked me why she hadn't died yet. "What's keeping me here? What do I still need to learn? Why doesn't God take me?" We hear variations of these same questions frequently. And, our answers are never adequate consolation. The woman asked specifically for some spiritual method that would help her to stop holding on so compulsively and allow her to surrender. She had a sincere feeling of gratitude for her life and felt confident that she would enter into a wonderful spiritual reality after death. But she feared having to squeeze through that narrow and unknown constriction of death. She feared having to 'lose it' completely and utterly. This body's faithful physical functioning and this mind's thinking and remembering had sustained her sense of personal continuity and identity. She asked what will happen to my 'me' without my body and mind.

She and I searched together for a meditative focus that would help to calm her mind. She was so easily distracted that it had to be something that was always there and unmistakable. It was discovered that she was very proud of her ability to breath deep and very slow and go without taking a breath for extended periods of time. Perfect!

Focusing on the breath is the most essential technique used in traditional meditation practice. I encouraged her to just watch this deep breathing and to let these intervals of not breathing lengthen. Then I asked her to notice how delightful it was to allow the next breath in. It is best if we can enjoy living while we practice this art of dying. Eventually this physical breath will merge into the spiritual breath of God. Perhaps she may be able to say at the hour of her death what an old Christian desert ascetic was once heard to say when he died, "Now I sleep, but my heart is awake."[vii]

THERAPEUTIC MUSIC IN A "CURING" ENVIRONMENT

My husband, Dave, was diagnosed with prostate cancer when he was 65. The cancer was aggressive and the doctor recommended surgery as the most effective treatment to hopefully cure him of the cancer. The surgery would last approximately one and one-half hours and I wanted him to have his own music for the procedure. After all, research has shown that a person is more relaxed listening to therapeutic music, even under anesthesia, and comes out from anesthesia more quickly. So we prepared an iPod Shuffle with his choice of music, Bach's *Unaccompanied Cello Suites* and others. I had devised a scheme to get the iPod Shuffle to him as soon as he was wheeled into the Recovery Room. But as Dave was about to be wheeled off to surgery, I checked with the surgeon to make certain his music would be allowed in the Recovery Room. The surgeon smiled at me and said, "He can have his music in surgery if he wants it. I listen to music all the time when I am operating." With surprise, I asked what kind of music he listened to. "It depends on the mood I am in." What a perfect response! We clipped the iPod Shuffle onto Dave's surgical gown, put on his earphones and he was wheeled off to surgery. He declared that he was awake by the time he was taken to the Recovery Room and knew the exact time.

Chapter 3

The Early Journey

Learn, grow, embrace life
While we can - while we care.

HOSPICE AND THE HARP

The harp is a magical instrument which I discovered at the age of forty-two. The folk harp and the piano are very similar in many ways and I quickly figured out the similarities. Harp music and piano music look alike with treble clef, bass clef and key signatures. Your left hand plays the bass clef (accompaniment) and your right hand plays the treble clef (melody). But on the harp, you play vertically on the strings and on the piano you play horizontally on the keys. So in a few months, I was figuring this instrument out in relation to my experience playing the piano for decades. Then I began to read about therapeutic music through books such as *The Power of Music* by Joshua Leeds and *The Healing Musician* by Stella Benson.

BARBARA, MY INTRODUCTION TO HOSPICE

My first introduction to Hospice was with Barbara, a church friend of mine. Barbara sang in the church choir at the North Valley Presbyterian Church, where I was the organist. Not being a smoker and being only fifty-five years old, her diagnosis of lung cancer came as quite a surprise to all of us. And then the double surprise, the cancer was the virulent kind that "took no quarter." Barbara was suddenly thrust into the last few months of her life immediately after her diagnosis. The choir went to her house and sang to her. Shortly after that, in her last few days, she was taken to the in-patient unit of Presbyterian Hospice. Her husband asked me to come and play harp music. I was scared and curious. I had never been to a hospice unit before, but I went. I played at her bed-side. The hospice chaplain, Catherine, walked by and asked me to step outside when I finished playing. When I did, she asked if I would just come and play on the unit occasionally. What an opportunity to learn about therapeutic music and death and dying and all that stuff I had been so curious about. So I agreed, looking forward to a new experience, but not really knowing what that meant or what it might be.

The first time I went to the hospice unit, I very shyly asked the unit nurse if it would be all right just to tuck into an empty room across from the nurse's station and quietly play. As I played, I was surprised to find that people would come in the room to listen and to visit. Wow, what a surprise! Music was a common language that we could all speak - children, adults, grieving families and hospice personnel. My music had healing properties, too. Families could sit and listen and children could sing along with *Twinkle Twinkle, Little Star* and *The Barney Song*.

"Hospice is one of the few options of healthcare that focuses on both the patient's and their family's emotional, spiritual and physical well-being when a terminal diagnosis has been made. Hospice works to respect the wishes of terminally ill patients and focuses on making the most of each day. The concept focuses on providing quality time, rather than pursuing aggressive treatment that may be invasive or painful. Quality of life versus quantity of life becomes paramount. Hospice provides a special, one-on-one type of care for a person with a life-limiting illness with a focus on quality of life in the last months, weeks and days. Care is focused on a patient's right to dignity at a time when one may be dependent on others for personal care and activities of daily living. Hospice is about living. Support is provided to the patient's families and loved ones, with counseling services and bereavement plans with support groups.

Hospice creates a caregiver and caregiving family. Hospice is made up of an interdisciplinary team of a physician, registered nurse, nursing assistant, chaplain, social worker, volunteers and therapeutic musicians. All members are trained professionals. This team will advocate for the patient's right to be informed and to direct their own plan of care."[viii]

Hospice care is a type of care and philosophy of care that focuses on the palliation of a chronically ill, seriously ill or terminally ill patient's pain and symptoms and attends to their emotional and spiritual needs.[ix] Hospice work is a grief profession, a discipline that integrates spiritual, psychological, medical, musical and healing professions. All of us that do this work know going into it that the patient is going to die. As Forrest Gump once said, "Dyin' is just part of livin'." We work together as an interdisciplinary team to bring comfort and quality of life to a patient at the end of his or her life. The work can be very intense, yet, very powerful as many of these stories show. But we still grieve. At the beginning of each team meeting, time is allowed for hospice personnel to remember their patients who have recently passed. There may be funny remembrances, tears, poignant stories and tributes, yet, it is a way to honor our patients and ourselves as we work in this grief profession.

I had many varied experiences during the two years I played on the in-patient hospice unit. One day, Michael, a hospice nurse, asked me if I knew the song, *Wind beneath My Wings*. When I played it, he would get a far-away stare in his eyes. Finally, some days later, he told me that song was played at his partner's funeral. Once when there were several children visiting a family member, one of the aides asked me if I knew the *Hokey Pokey*. I started playing it and she formed a conga line with the children. They were all doing the *Hokey Pokey* down the hall. It was like a breath of fresh air to witness the children laughing and singing and being led by a hospice aide with a loving heart who understood the sadness of witnessing a grandparent die.

I was playing on the unit one day after Mother Theresa died. Catherine, the hospice chaplain, came on the unit and commented that she had heard me when she came in the front doors of the hospital. She sat down on the floor beside me and started quietly weeping. Catherine was a former Catholic nun and I think she was grieving the loss of Mother Theresa. She sat weeping for a while then, got up and went on about her work. I still reflect on that experience. She obviously needed to grieve, found a comfortable space in which to do it and then went on with her work. I took that to be a wonderful compliment and commentary on the power of music.

Chapter 4

All about the Journey, Not the Destination

*A privilege and honor
To accompany them part way
On their final journey.*

Going Away Concerts

I have played the harp for many of what I call "Going Away Concerts." Each experience of playing music therapeutically for a dying person has contributed to the beauty and wonder I feel in having the privilege of helping these individuals pass over.

Charlotte's Church Friend

Charlotte called me late one evening and asked me to go see her church friend. When I arrived, the church family was gathered around the bed. The patient had some discomfort, as she kept trying to change positions and to sit up in bed. The music quickly evolved into a going away concert by the church family. As the music continued, the singing got stronger and I became secondary to what was going on. After the members exhausted all the hymns I knew, they began singing hymns specific to their church. Would you believe, they all pulled out iPhones and started pulling up the lyrics of hymns so as to continue singing! The patient relaxed, laid back down and really enjoyed her concert. What a joy to see caring people join their voices, their love and their energy to comfort and love someone into another space.

SHIRLEY'S JUST NOT READY

A hospice chaplain called me a few days before Christmas to tell me that Shirley was actively dying, the family had gathered and she was not expected to make it through the night. Could I stop by? Of course I can. After all, this is my work. As I sit in the room with the family, I begin very quietly entraining with Shirley's breathing. She really appears to be on her journey. Her favorite grandson is holding her hand and tells her how lovely her nails look (an aide had just painted them for her). And then, a little ninety plus year old lady with dementia came into the room and started flirting with Shirley's grandson. Oops, not a good idea, remember, hearing is the last sense to go and this was Shirley's favorite grandson. The little lady wanders out, yet Shirley has heard and taken notice. And, she wakes up. Needless to say, everyone is quite startled. This one doesn't play according to the script. And then, Shirley announces that she's hungry for oatmeal and a donut! Everyone looks at me since I'm the official hospice person and wonders what to do. I suggest that one of them run to the grocery store and get her a donut. Meanwhile, I check in with the hospice nurse who is slightly amazed. We hold the cell phone up to Shirley's ear and she and the nurse visit briefly. Shirley seems to have returned from the almost-dead. The family requests a bit more up-beat music. We all visit, I play some country western music and Shirley is brought some food. A few days later, the family gave her a Christmas party and I stopped by to play some Christmas music. What a blast! There's Shirley sitting in the living area of the hospice unit, enjoying her family, has her hair fixed and has a few gifts. Would you believe it, Shirley stayed with us for a couple of months after that. There's simply no predicting the human spirit.

JOSE AND HIS FAMILY

Before I tell you about Jose, let me share the prelude music of Adelita, his wife. I had been to see her in January at a local nursing home. They had a large Hispanic family with a two-month old baby, three little girls and a grandson Joseph, who was a musician. There was lots of activity and noise and it was wonderful! Adelita soon passed away. Five months later, Jose's daughter asked me to come see her dad at the same nursing home. Now, it was her dad that was actively dying. Was it from a broken heart? Sometimes it happens. When I arrived, there were eight great grandchildren aged five to eleven in the room around the bed and five or more adults. They were a large, loving family paying tribute to the patron of the family. I suggested that the little ones sing to great grandpa, songs such as *Twinkle, Twinkle* and *The Barney Song*. What a beautiful sight! They crawled up on the bed to be close to him, I struck up the harp and we sang. And the adults started singing! After a few songs, the youngsters lost interest, got off the bed and wandered off. But the adults wanted or needed to sing and so we gave great grandpa a wonderful, emotionally rousing going away concert. What a way to go! We should all be so lucky to have our family with us and singing their favorite songs.

ADELE THE ROCK STAR

WOW! A total rock star, what a lady! Adele had been a school superintendent in several major metropolitan school districts. A warrior for children, her bulldozer management style unsettled union leaders and politicians as noted in her obituary in the New York Times. Actively dying at sixty-six years old, her family gave her a wonderful going away concert. As I entered her bedroom, one daughter was on the bed singing golden oldie hymns. I quietly sat at the foot of the bed and started playing hymns with her. As we sang and played, other family members came in. A son came in, knelt by the bed-side and read some scriptures. Then, more singing and praying. The image in my mind is one of a beautiful, loving family of strong faith singing good-bye to their mother. Over a year after her passing, I saw

DONESE MAYFIELD

her son at a sports event. We visited and fondly remembered the beautiful sacred moment of the family singing good-bye to their mother.

Jan's Dad, Roger, and His Singing Family

Jan's dad, Roger, was on the in-patient hospice unit at Presbyterian Hospital. The family had gathered and I had been asked to join them. As I played, I heard various family members humming. Then someone quietly asked if I knew *Jesus Loves Me*. As I began to play, people started to quietly sing and soon, the singing escalated. This was a family who loved to sing and this family needed to give Dad a going away concert. I played and they sang all the old hymns. WOW, what a tribute! When we ran out of hymns that we knew from memory, Rita, a hospice aide, brought us an old hymnal. And, we played and sang more songs, creating a truly fitting send-off by a loving family who needed to sing. Oh, and by the way, the family noticed dad's feet moving in time to the music under the sheet. He was there with us, he heard the singing and enjoyed every moment of it. Oh, the power of music!

Singers need to sing and love to sing. Singing can be therapeutic. As mentioned earlier, music is stored in a different part of the brain from speech. Oftentimes, non-verbal dementia and Alzheimer's patients will hear the strains of a familiar song and join in! This has happened so frequently that I am no longer surprised by it. *You Are My Sunshine* is an all-time favorite. Everyone seems to know and love this song and they love to sing it especially when I comment that I only "make a joyful noise" and my vocal cords really are in my fingers. As soon as I begin, people really, really want to join me and do, even the ones who don't remember speech. I tell them that it's okay if we don't remember the words. We can just make them up. And if we don't make up the words, we can hum. Everyone catches on and gets in the spirit of joyful noise making! It is amazing to see. What a thrill it gives me every time I witness the joy and power of music.

Chapter 5

OLD MUSICIANS DON'T DIE,
WE JUST DECOMPOSE

*Musicians feel and hear - with a
different set of ears - our reality.*

The following are stories of patients I have played for who had an avid interest in music. Their stories demonstrate the healing power of music!

RIO RANCHO ROGER

As I played for Roger, he was making some very strange noises in his throat.

I happened to be playing *Over the Rainbow* at the time and I was concerned that he was having some type of discomfort. He also seemed to be moving his feet. I very carefully watch the patient to see any change in breathing, facial response and slight movement of the hands or feet. Oftentimes, I can read pain in the patient's face. Sometimes, I can sense anxiety or agitation in their slight body movement. His daughters were gathered by his bed-side. I looked at them to get their reactions. They both smiled and said to me, "Daddy is trying to sing with you. He was a radio announcer and a singer!" The power of music is amazing!

LIL AND MUSCLE MEMORY

Lil was a long-time music teacher who had music in her soul. She was in the memory care unit at a local nursing home. When her children would sit her down at the piano, her hands would still attempt to play up and down the keyboard. This is called muscle memory. "Muscle memory has been used synonymously with motor learning, which is a form of procedural memory that involves consolidating a specific motor task into memory through repetition. When a movement is repeated over time, a long-term muscle memory is created for that task, eventually allowing it to be performed without conscious effort. This process decreases the need for attention and creates maximum efficiency within the motor and memory systems. Examples of muscle memory are found in many everyday activities that become automatic and improve with practice, such as riding a bicycle, typing on a keyboard, typing in a PIN or playing a melody or phrase on a musical instrument."[x]

One day, I went to visit Lil and she was in the living room with several other residents. I sat down with them and began to play some of the golden oldies songs such as *You Are My Sunshine, My Bonnie Lies over the Ocean* and *She'll Be Coming 'Round the Mountain*. As I watched Lil, she was smiling and singing with us. When I finished playing, I went over to tell her what fun it had been to have her join us. She looked me directly in the eyes, reached over, brushed some hair from my cheek and told me how much she enjoyed it! A moment of total clarity and then she was gone again into her other world. This is frequently the situation with dementia patients - a brief moment of clarity and then gone somewhere else.

A few weeks later, Lil had to have a minor procedure done with a local anesthetic. Her family asked me to be with her and the medical staff as they did the minor operation. I played music to calm her while the physician did the procedure. As I watched the activity, I realized that the music calmed the entire room. The energy changed. I was asked if I happened to know various songs. This is what I call "Stump the Musician." It can be a lot of fun for the player and the listeners. And it can bring comfort and peace to all who are involved. I laughingly tell people that I play everything from Bach to The Beatles. If I don't know a particular song requested, I suggest something in a similar genre. That usually works.

LUCILLE, ALWAYS A TEACHER

Lucille is an elderly music teacher. I've been to see her several times. She's "there." One time she became very interested in my harp. She wanted to know if it was a chromatic instrument. I explained to her that it was basically chromatic with a potential diatonic "twist." This is stuff that only musicians understand, let alone have any concern about! But she was so interested and kept watching me as I played. She asked several times if it was chromatic. Here is an overly simplified explanation of chromatic and diatonic for those who might be interested. We might think of diatonic as the white notes on the piano keyboard and chromatic as the white notes plus the black notes. The Celtic style harp that I play is mostly diatonic, but I can make occasional black notes by raising a lever on a string. This shortens the vibrating length so as to raise the tone of the string by one-half step. So you might see why few, if any, hospice patients would care about this, except old musicians!

THERESA, SHE'S IN THERE AND WE BOTH KNOW IT

Theresa is one hundred and four years of age and had been the organist and choir director at a Catholic church in the Valley. In her family home, she had a grand piano, a small Wurlitzer organ, an old Celtic harp and an interesting zither on the mantle. I looked up the zither in an instrument book to see what it was after my first visit there. The next time I went to visit Theresa, she was slumped over in a chair in the sun room with that "gaze into another place" look in one eye. The other eye was rolled back in her head. I sat down close to her and began to play. I watched her very closely as I played. I played a variety of music, some old hymns, a bit of Gregorian chant and I even sang a little. Very slowly, Theresa's gaze returned to this world. Her eyes focused. I knew she was in there. Then, I saw her move her gaze directly to me. She watched me. Then, she smiled! Her daughter was totally amazed and so was I. She said it was the most responsive Theresa had been in two to three days. I moved the harp closer to her and she actually raised her hand and touched the strings. It was a profound musical and spiritual experience with Theresa. She and I were somewhere together for a while with music as the channel and connection. It took me a while to get re-grounded after that experience.

Theresa's obituary noted, "...A defining element in Theresa's life was the loss of her five siblings in one night to the influenza epidemic which swept the world in the winter of 1918-1919. She was the sole survivor at age nine. Early in her life, Theresa demonstrated an interest in music and learned to play the piano. She graduated high school in Pueblo where she provided the graduation music and provided music when she graduated in public health nursing at Case Western Reserve University."

ALMA, DETERMINED TO PLAY THE HARP!

Alma was a young woman in her early fifties dying of breast cancer. She was totally fascinated with the harp. A harp student of mine who was also a hospice volunteer started visiting Alma on a regular basis at the nursing home. They had fun together as they made music, sang and visited. Alma wanted to play the harp, but she couldn't rest the small harp on her shoulder to be able to pull the strings. So Billie, the volunteer, brought a small pentatonic harp that would rest on Alma's lap. Alma could strum the strings or pluck individual strings. The harp had eleven strings but only five tones in each octave, thus, the name penta-tonic harp. Alma wanted to have a Little Minstrel harp of her own, but she had no resources to buy one. And, so she managed to beg, borrow and do whatever it took to get the money to acquire a harp. And she got one! I have no idea how she scraped together the several hundred dollars to purchase the harp and I didn't want to know. She played that harp until her final days. What a strong will and spirit. Life is short, eat dessert first!

Chapter 6

None of Us Has a Lease on Life

*The beauty of life seen in so many
small ways - hugs, tears, care, love.*

We all make our life transition at some point on our journey. And, I have found through my experience as a therapeutic musician that music creates a bridge to the other world that eases the passage into the unknown. In the following stories, I share the beauty of the present moment and strength of the human spirit as I recount playing for patients and families when it's time to cross over.

ILA, THE MARK WE LEAVE ON THE WORLD
Ila was thirty-two years old when he passed away. He developed Batten's disease, a progressive neurological disorder,

when he was quite young. I only met him on the last day of his life when a mutual friend of mine and his mother's asked me to be with him. The staff at the group home for the developmentally disabled where Ila had lived for several years cautioned me about Ila. They told me he might become agitated with the music and might react negatively. I assured them that I monitored a person's reaction very closely and adjusted music accordingly or even stopped if necessary. As I began to play, Ila's mother, the group home manager and a minister who was a close friend, were by his bed. They all observed that his breathing calmed almost immediately. I stayed long enough to see that the breathing change continued. The manager then asked if I would go out in the living room and play for some of the residents and I did. Ila passed away later that day.

JOSHUA WITH PICK'S DISEASE

Pick's disease is a rare neuro-degenerative disease that causes progressive destruction of nerve cells in the brain. Symptoms include loss of speech and dementia. Joshua, or JoJo as he was called, was a young twenty-two year old Native American who had been moved in from the reservation for his final chapter of life. The day I visited him, the apartment was filled with several female family members who were keeping the family vigil. Oftentimes, families feel that they need to be with the dying member continuously. The person should not die alone. Other cultures and traditions feel differently. Some feel the dying person should be left alone to do his "final work." A Hospice Team member notes, "I've had many private conversations over the years with dying people in which they've shared their fears. Often they're afraid of suffering. They fear for their families' well-being and, sometimes, they worry that they've left some piece of interpersonal work undone. But they never tell me they fear dying alone. On the contrary, some have said they were afraid of dying in front of their families. They wanted to spare them the pain of witnessing that final breath."[xi]

All hospice veterans have seen this - a family sits in vigil with a loved one who seems endlessly suspended between life and death. Then, the family leaves perhaps to get a bite to eat. And moments after the loved ones exit, the dying person completes the work and the soul detaches from the body. When families express amazement, we tend to offer an interpretation. "She was waiting for you all to leave," we say, "probably because she wanted to protect you from seeing the very end." And this explanation, in my experience, is comforting to families. We say that no one should die alone, yet we seem to accept with equanimity when someone we love - and I hesitate to use this word - chooses to die alone. It's an odd paradox. Perhaps the dying don't fear dying alone. Perhaps on some level they embrace it. And so perhaps what we ought to say is not that no one should die alone, but that no one should have to because of circumstance or fate.

KATIE, SO LOVED

Oh, yes, Katie, she was a fifty-eight year old woman with Down's syndrome and Alzheimer's. Down's syndrome is a genetic disorder caused by the presence of an extra copy of the chromosome trisomy-21. Down's syndrome is the most common chromosome abnormality in humans. The following is taken from her obituary. "If you enter this world knowing you are loved and you leave this world knowing the same, then everything that happens in between can be dealt with." When the hospice chaplain called me, he mentioned that my playing would likely be for the caregivers. When I arrived, Katie was actively dying and there were two of her caregivers who had been with her for many years. They both talked about Katie. They told me how she loved to dance and how she adored everything about weddings, the cake, the dress, the music and the flowers. "She could tell you every detail of her perfect wedding, except for the groom, whom she didn't seem to be too particular about." They showed me a picture of Katie in her Wonder Woman costume. It was on their cell phones. And then they asked me to play wedding music for Katie. Of course, I played all the traditional wedding music I knew. The caregivers cried and grieved. They moved to the living room to allow me some time alone with Katie to work with her breathing. After a while, her breathing calmed. I had finished my work and went to the living room to spend more time with the caregivers. They cried more and I did, too. Katie was loved and she knew it at some level. What a beautiful experience for us all.

JACKIE AND HER HOSPICE FAMILY

Jackie, a sixty year old, three hundred pound plus woman with chronic heart failure and multiple complications, was a very complex person. She had a lot of anxiety and a lot of anger towards her family. Life was an increasingly difficult process for her. I first went to see Jackie in her tiny, cluttered apartment at the social worker's request. Jackie was anxious, fidgety and asked for some quiet music. I began to play some lullabies and she settled down and immediately went to sleep. Mission accomplished for the time being. I visited her several times at her apartment and met her mother and sister. She always wanted quiet, calming music and would then settle down and fall sleep.

Then, I heard Jackie tried to commit suicide. Now, it is not uncommon for hospice patients to talk about suicide or even ask hospice personnel to help them end their lives. This final stage of life can be difficult, challenging and painful. But Jackie actually tried so the hospice team worked together to place her in a nursing home facility where she would get more continuous care and monitoring. Sadly, there had been so much drama and unhappiness in Jackie's life, especially in her final months. I visited Jackie several more times at the facility. We had enjoyable conversations and she always wanted me to play music, everything from country western to The Beatles to old hymns and lullabies. And she always settled and slept. The last visit I had with Jackie, unbeknownst to me, was the day she died. The social worker called to tell me that Jackie was declining. I happened to be going in the general area of the nursing home, so I decided to stop in. Jackie wasn't very responsive. But I stayed with her long enough to see her breathing calm down and a look of peacefulness come into her face. She passed a short while after I left her. Her hospice team, including me, was left with a good memory of her passing.

"Grumpy" Bob

What an interesting person! Bob was sixty-eight years old, dying of lung cancer and, yes, he was a long-time smoker and pissed at the world in general. For some unknown reason, he grudgingly agreed to allow me to visit him. When I arrived, he sat in his recliner, smoking and watching me. I sat off to one side in my small folding chair. I opened up my harp and began a conversation with him. "What kind of music do you like?" I asked. "I play everything from Bach to The Beatles," I offered. We agreed on some Beatles tunes and I began to play. From there, we moved to country western. This genre generally surprises people when they hear *Your Cheatin' Heart* by Hank Williams on the harp followed by *King of the Road* by Roger Miller. Those tunes are usually ice breakers. This all led to a discussion of theology. Bob told me he last visited an Episcopal church many years ago and had given up on religion. I told him I was Episcopalian by tradition but totally understood his abandonment of organized religion, one point we agreed on! Moving on, I told him I recently visited the Unitarian Universalist church and found it to be very similar to Christianity without the Christ figure. So interestingly, we non-theologians engaged in a conversation about theology, a conversation in which we found many points of agreement.

Bob then told me he had run off a hospice social worker and chaplain. They just didn't fit the bill for him. I understood. Sometimes younger hospice workers, though they have a wonderfully compassionate spirit, just don't have the life experiences of us older individuals. Bob then asked if I was able to play some improvisational type music without specific melodies. Of course, this is my real work. I just do The Beatles and pop stuff to entertain and open a communication channel. At some level, Bob and I connected as mature, intelligent beings and he allowed me into his more private space. What a meaningful experience for both of us.

PAUL, FOREVER YOUNG

Paul was a professional soccer player, twenty-nine years old, with amyotrophic lateral sclerosis (ALS). A family friend asked me to be with the family, but Paul passed before I could get there and so I assumed that I was not needed. But then Paul's brother called me a few hours later. He asked me to be with the family until the body was transported. And so, I went to the house where Paul and all the family, his parents, grandparents, girlfriend, brothers, etc. had gathered. Paul was still in the bedroom in his wheelchair as I played music in the living room. There was lots of food and spirits, family visiting, sharing stories, crying and laughing. I played Irish music at the request of his Mom, who was Irish, and lullabies for other family members. Then, they brought Paul out in his wheelchair. Everyone said their goodbyes. It was so sad.

The funeral home employees took him outside to put him on the gurney and transport him and I was also asked to go outside. After Paul was gone, the family returned to the house and so did I at their request. The family asked for the song *Forever Young* and we talked about how Paul will always be young in their memories.

> May the good Lord be with you, down every road you
> roam
> And may sunshine and happiness surround you when
> you're far from home
> And may you grow to be proud, dignified and true
> And do unto others as you'd have done to you
> Be courageous and be brave and in my heart you'll al-
> ways stay
> Forever young, Forever young[xii]

I played *The Parting Glass*, an old Irish drinking song, and explained the context.

> Oh, all the money that e're I spent,
> I spent it in good company,
> And all the harm that e're I've done,
> Alas it was to none but me,
> And all I've done for want of wit
> To mem'ry now I can't recall.
> So fill to me the parting glass,
> Good night, and joy be with you all.

Oh, all the comrades that e're I had,
Are sorry for my going away,
And all the sweethearts that e're I had
Would wish me one more day to stay.
But since it falls unto my lot
That I should rise and you should not,
I'll gently rise and softly call,
"Good night, and joy be with you all."

As I left, I had a big hole in my heart for the family and for Paul who will be forever young in everyone's hearts.

Chapter 7

SOMETIMES WE CAN PICK OUR TIME OF DEPARTURE

Choice - a strange, scary and uplifting idea
Control? Really? WOW!

THIN PLACES

"In the Celtic Christian tradition, there is much mention of thin places or a thin veil. A thin place is one where the seen and unseen intersect, the eternal and the temporal co-mingle and the divine suffuses the earthly realm with the whisper of God's creation blessing, "This is all very good." Oftentimes, a thin place is a tangible location, a piece of creation, like the Isle of Iona or Ghost Ranch in New Mexico. Sometimes, thin places are events in life where the sacred seems very close at hand. The birth of a child, the joy at a glad reunion, luminous worship, the love of a life companion, the sense of community among a people committed to some great thing and the holy mystery of death."[xiii]

I have come to believe in the portability of thinness. When I'm bedside with an actively dying patient, I seem to go in and out of thinness a great deal. I breathe with the patient. I match their breathing pattern with music, working in different musical modes to find what resonates with them and watching for signs of pain and/or anxiety.

Often times, when a patient is actively dying, we are held in a circle that comprises a thin place. There is an intersection of life and death, of sacred and secular, of spiritual and temporal. Sometimes, family members may be uncomfortable with some of their loved one's behaviors. Frequently, in the last few days, even weeks, the patient will visit with family members who have passed away before them. They will then come back to this reality and comment on Mom or Dad or Uncle Joe or Aunt Sue who had been in the room with them. Sometimes, the patient will see angels in the room and then comment about it. Oftentimes, in their final days, they will have what appears to be a blank stare in their eyes, looking somewhere that we can't see. I tell their family members that I believe they are actually seeing into the next reality or place where they are going. We can't see it because we are not as far along on our journey as they are. After all, we are all on this life journey at different places along the way. And that thin veil? Well, the patient is looking through the veil to the other side.

There is much to know about life and the human spirit. We have much more control over our lives than we are taught or understand. Here are several heart-warming stories of individuals who made the decision as to when they would leave this life.

PEG, DON'T SPOIL CHRISTMAS

Peg was a fifty-four year old woman with lymphoma. It was Christmas time. I had been to see her and her family several times shortly before Christmas. After I visited and played music with her in her bedroom, the priest anointed her. I went in the living room and played Christmas music for the family. What a difficult situation. I didn't have words to comfort, and sometimes the comfort simply comes from music. Peg was very strong-willed and waited until after Christmas to die so as not to spoil the family holiday and leave sad holiday memories for her family.

FLORENCE, FOREVER THE MOM

Florence was in a small group home. She was tenacious about life, but her body had just simply worn out. Hospice staff just scratched their heads and cared for her as best they could. I had visited her on Saturday and the following Tuesday. She was in there, in what was left of her body. She made eye contact with me with one eye several times as I played for her. She was teaching me, I just had to figure out what. Then, I learned from the staff that she had a daughter in another nursing home with an incurable illness. Florence was concerned about the daughter. Of course, we mothers never quit caring for and about our children, even when they are taking care of us! We had to find a way to tell Florence her daughter would be all right and she could go on. Finally, as I played, I talked to her. I told her I understood her care and concern because I was a mother. You never quit worrying and caring about your children. That's just part of our job. But it was okay. We mothers always care about our children's well-being and her daughter was well cared for. I assured her of that several times. Florence passed the next day.

CHUCK AND CLAIRE

Sometimes, elderly couples are both on hospice service at the same time. This was the situation with Chuck and Claire. They were part of a large, effusive Italian family. When I went to visit Chuck on Monday, he was actively dying and Claire was sitting in a wheelchair next to his bed. I visited with her and played some of her and Chuck's favorite music. The house was full of people and food. Twins run in the family and there were three or four sets of twins, from babies to adults. They asked me to return the next day. And, when I did, Chuck was very actively dying by this time. He died shortly after that. Claire passed away twenty hours later. When I heard, I stopped by to take a plant and visit the grieving family. Claire must have died of a broken heart. The family told me that she just threw up her hands and passed away.

Inez and Homer

Inez and Homer were on hospice together at an assisted living facility. They were in a room together with their beds next to each other. Homer would ask, "Momma, are you there?" And the daughter who was with them would reply, "Yes, Dad, she's here. Wave at Dad, Momma!" Momma would raise her arm up to wave at Dad and they'd both settle down, content to know each was there. Well, Homer passed in April. I went back in June to see Inez. Sure enough, she passed shortly after my visit in June. She missed Homer and went to be with him.

Aurora, A Spontaneous Rosary

Aurora's husband had passed a few days before I was called by the hospice chaplain to visit Aurora. The family home was small and completely filled with family members. Some family members even overflowed onto the patio. There was lots of activity, talking and buzzing around. Aurora was in a hospital bed in one corner of the living room. The hospice chaplain presented Aurora with a prayer shawl knitted by our hospice volunteers, a gesture of kindness and love. The chaplain recited some Bible verses and said a prayer and, somehow, a spontaneous rosary began. Now, the chaplain was not Catholic, but the family was and everyone immediately settled down, got quiet and became reverent. The energy in the room changed and even Aurora sensed the change. What a beautiful experience and what a privilege to be part of it. Aurora went on to be with her husband shortly after that.

BETTY

Betty was a developmentally disabled thirty-seven year old woman. She had a genetic defect referred to as Chromosome 14. She was a beautiful, tiny person with dark hair, eyebrows and eye lashes and weighed thirty-two pounds. She and her brother, Teddy, also with a Chromosome 14 defect, had been adopted by a couple some years ago. They were family. Teddy and Betty had been loved and cared for all these years by their adoptive parents. Teddy had died a very difficult death last year. The police were involved, even though Teddy had been on hospice (a different hospice from the one I am with). It was sad, tragic and unnecessary. Our hospice staff explained all of this to me when they asked me to go see the family. I went, I played and I visited with Betty's mom, Joan. Joan told me she had loved and cared for Betty and Teddy all of her adult life. She didn't know what she would do without them. I comforted her as best I could and assured her she would figure it out in time. Grief will find completion if you allow yourself to work through the process. The time with Betty and Joan was one of those sacred moments of thinness that just, sometimes, spontaneously happens. It was a very profound and meaningful time that I spent with this family.

And then, a few weeks later, I played at a memorial service for a family I knew. As I was playing the after-service music while the family and friends were leaving, I noticed a woman sitting quietly to the side watching and waiting. It was

Betty's mother, Joan. She joined me and we visited. Betty had passed and her service had been a few days ago. Joan and I sat, hugged, cried and visited for quite some time. That veil was very thin. We were meant to be there together, it was no coincidence. Oh, the portability of thinness.

Chapter 8

NOT ALL WHO WANDER ARE LOST

A half-full glass - life is good
Be grateful in all things - easier said than done.

ALICE'S JOURNEY

Alice is walking her own, sometimes scary, journey with Lewy-Body dementia (LBD). She refers to the diagnosis as "this brain thing I have." (LBD is the second most common type of dementia, with an estimated 1.3 million Americans diagnosed. Symptoms and memory can vary significantly in LBD, such that on one day your relative might not recognize you and the next day, she can recall the names of each of her grandchildren. Visual hallucinations, where people see things that are not actually there, are quite common in LBD.)[xiv]

A long-time friend who got me into hospice work many years ago once wisely counseled me about Alzheimer and dementia patients with this succinct phrase, "You dance their dance." If a patient tells me the sky is purple, I respond by saying, "That is the prettiest purple I have ever seen." In other words, you go into their reality with them. This can be an interesting journey with someone who is hallucinating. Alice, for example, had some imaginary friends and pets in the corner of her living room. When she asked if I could see them, I truthfully answered that I could not, but I also comforted her by saying that I think it is really fun to have some imaginary friends and pets. What a delightful idea! After all, many of us had imaginary playmates when we were young - so why not when we are old? Alice described them to me and we laughed. And I gave her a hug. I danced her dance and it was fun for both of us and comforting to her. Alice was sometimes scared because she recognized that her reality was oftentimes different from ours. Hugs can say so much that words cannot.

SPIRITUAL INSIGHTS FROM A PASTOR WHO HAD ALZHEIMER'S DISEASE

"My journey into Alzheimer's is a valuable resource for those wishing to understand and attempt to meet the spiritual needs of people with Alzheimer's disease,"[xv] notes author Robert Davis. With help from his wife, Davis documented how Alzheimer's disease changed his life. Davis went from experiencing the sunlight of a close relationship to God to a dim moonlight and, sometimes, feelings of total blackness. The feelings of joy and peace, the times of love and worship and the tender personal relationships Davis had known all his life, were gone. The concept of a relationship with God became hard to mentally process even for this man who had been the spiritual leader of a huge, growing church in Miami, Florida.

As one who had never really known fear, it was his unaccountable fear that Davis noticed first. He could no longer recall comforting memories or mind-sustaining Bible verses. "The sweetness of prayer and the gentle comfort of the Holy Spirit had disappeared",[xvi] noted Davis. Reverend Davis understood firsthand why established Christians suddenly weep and cry because they are afraid that God doesn't love them anymore or that they have lost their faith or that they will somehow miss going to heaven. Davis felt that individuals with Alzheimer's disease often experienced spiritual torture. Davis wrote, "This is a time for comfort, reassurance, a soft touch and a gentle voice with soothing words or even songs if you are so gifted. Whatever body language speaks peace in your family can be put to good use in this situation. As soon as my wife is aware that I am in one of these states, she embraces me and strokes me. She asks me to tell her about what is bothering me. As I talk about it, the panic subsides and I am made aware that I am in touch with reality again and that I am once more saved from the black hole."[xvii]

As the disease progressed, Davis could not sustain spiritual nourishment from the usual channels of prayer, meditation and Bible study. Yet, he was often surprised by thoughts and Bible verses that would pop into his mind. Davis enjoyed these thoughts and praised God for them as long as he could.

Bringing Spiritual Comfort to those with Dementia

We can enjoy music with the withdrawn resident. Simply draw close to the face of a withdrawn person and sing softly into their ear. Take their hand and gently move it with the rhythm of the music. Often the person will awaken from her trance and smile or laugh. Moyra Jones writes, "Music, art, nonverbal stimuli and similar experiential approaches become paramount for establishing and maintaining connections and relationships in the now or spiritual moment. Caregivers, family members and others need to focus on the moment of being connected and not expect to be either remembered or anticipated. The effects of these interactions, however, do remain. The glow of spiritual wellness derived from sharing the present moment continues on. Even after the visitor is gone, the visitor's gift of being fully present may still provide strength and spiritual nourishment to the person with dementia. Finally, the use of deep-seated and long-learned poems, music, religious litera-ture and other items can trigger a sense of spiritual wellness in the person with dementia."[xviii]

Chapter 9

INTERESTING AND DIFFERENT
CELEBRATIONS OF LIFE

"Who am I to judge?"

POPE FRANCIS

IRENE'S IRISH WAKE

Irene celebrated her one hundredth birthday in high style with neighbors and friends stopping by to wish her well. When I arrived to play, I sat right next to Irene so we could visit. Nothing doing, Irene wanted Irish music and she wanted to sing. So we sang lots of good Irish songs! A few months later, Irene passed and her daughter asked me to play her wake. At the funeral home, I sat in the corner opposite the open casket. Irene looked lovely and very much at peace. Somehow, she even looked younger than the last time I had seen her. This is not uncommon when death removes the pain and weight of this life. Family and friends began to arrive, lots and lots of them. They filled the room. They viewed and visited with Irene. And, then, one of them came to me to ask if I knew a country western song, which I did. Next thing you know, a quartet was singing and I was playing. What fun! Good friends, good conversation and good music. The only thing missing was setting Irene up in the casket and putting a glass of Irish whiskey in her hand. I was told that they do that some-times at Irish wakes!

Music Comforts the Living, Not the Dead

I have played for quite a few memorials, obviously, because of the hospice work I do and also because I play the piano, organ and harp. I can play a variety of music on whichever instru-ment is appropriate. Jim had been ill for quite some time and, as he declined, he mapped out the music he wanted for his memorial which was to take place in a traditional Presbyterian church. It included the songs *The Entertainer*, *The Gambler*, and *Take Me Back to Indiana*. The minister was not comfortable with the selections, yet, he was gracious to honor the family's requests. And, I filled in for the musician. I have to assume that Jim was from Indiana or had some very fond memories of that state. *The Gambler*, well, who knows? I can only guess. However, when I finished playing *The Entertainer* on the pia-no, I glanced down at the family in the front row. His daughter looked up at me, smiled and quietly applauded. Right on! I felt as though I had hit one out of the ball park!

Then, I was asked to play at a memorial service at a private home. The deceased's grown children asked me to play *Ain't Misbehavin'* on the harp! Tricky, but when I got through with it, everyone applauded. I still wonder why that particular song! It had some significance that only the insider family seemed to understand. And, then, I was asked to play *Pomp and Circumstance* for an elderly lady's service at a Presbyterian church. Why? And then it occurred to me, she had graduated from this life and that was the song she had requested to be played at her graduation! How cool!

CHURCH OF THE GOLDEN CORRAL

Patrick had Alzheimer's disease and lived in a group home. His wife visited him every day and took him to lunch at the Golden Corral buffet several times a week. They considered it their second home. When he was actively dying, I visited him and played some Irish music, which he heard in his own way. After he passed, his wife decided to have his memorial at the Golden Corral. After all, that was where they ate several times a week and they knew the employees. So we planned his memorial there. Our chaplain did a review of Patrick's life before retirement. Songs including *When Irish Eyes Are Smiling*, *Danny Boy* and others were sung and then everyone ate lunch and shared anecdotes of Patrick. What a joyful celebration of Patrick's life!

HANK'S BEDSIDE MEMORIAL

Hank seemed to be actively dying when I arrived, though he showed none of the typical signs of imminent death such as agitation or pain or strange breathing patterns. He just appeared to be quietly sleeping. Though I was playing music for Hank, his wife wanted to visit with me. She talked about a German zither that had been in her family for decades. Then, within ten minutes of the beginning of the music, Hank's breathing changed. Shortly after that, he smiled and his color changed and, then, he was gone. It was a sacred moment. What a beautiful death. After hospice was called and the nursing home staff took care of the official business of death, a bedside memorial was conducted for staff and residents. What a beautiful event. The room was crowded with people, it was standing room only. The chaplain recited a brief service and I played hymns. Everyone had the opportunity to tell Hank goodbye in their own way. And I will have the memory of his smile as he passed on.

A MEMORIAL FOR FAMILIES

I thought it a bit strange when I was asked to play for a memorial service at the University of New Mexico Alumni Chapel. Now, I understand and play many memorial services of every persuasion imaginable. Yet, this one was for the families of individuals who had donated their bodies to the University of New Mexico Medical School. These bodies had been designated and used for medical research. Many, many thoughts went through my mind as I considered what this service might be like.

I was asked to play harp music at the beginning of the service as guests and families arrived. Then, various medical students made their offerings of music and poetry. Some presented poems written from their hearts. Others presented traditional poetry. Some of the medical students presented music that was very tastefully and professionally done. What a gift to the families. All in all, it was a very meaningful, touching service conducted to honor those who had donated their bodies to medical research. The service and offerings validated the worthiness of this noble gift to the families left behind.

RESPECT ALL CULTURES

Eleanor had been brought in from the reservation to her daughter's home. Her daughter was the primary caregiver, though when I was there, several family members were present. I sat directly in front of Eleanor and played various kinds of music. Eleanor was blind yet, she wanted to touch the harp. Being a small, twenty-six string lap harp, I was able to hold it in front of her so that she could see the instrument in her own way. We had a lovely visit. As I prepared to leave, the daughters gave me a gift, a brown paper sack with several pieces of fruit in it. I normally do not accept gifts from hospice families yet, something told me to accept it, be gracious and say thank you. Later, I learned that it was a Native American practice to offer a gift in return for a gift. It is a lovely custom and one I have experienced several times since then from Native Americans. How gracious.

A few months later, I was asked to play at Eleanor's service on the reservation. What an honor! I drove to a small Presbyterian church on the reservation having no idea what to expect. It was a beautiful blended service of Native American and Christian customs. The service was conducted in both Pueblo and English. I played at the end of the service as friends and family came to the open casket to pay their respects. When everyone was through, family members sprinkled the deceased with corn pollen and covered her with a Native American blanket. The casket was then closed and moved to the church courtyard where she was laid to rest. What an honor and privilege to be part of a blended farewell to Eleanor.

Chapter 10

AND THE JOURNEY CONTINUES...

Death is not the end
No way
Butterflies, dreams, rainbows...

From this journey I have been on for the past years, I have learned many lessons, but several very important lessons stand out.

Lesson One - I am going to die. I don't know when or how, but it is guaranteed that I am going to die. This is not a great surprise to me from all the work with hospice patients I have done over the past decades. And yet, so many people are in denial about their eventual demise. Why is that so? Why is it such a surprise when the body parts begin to fail, eye sight and hearing begin to fade and skin wrinkles? It is all part of the aging process that we all go through if we live long enough.

Barbara Karnes, RN, in a booklet called *A Time to Live* frames this decline of life in such a beautiful way, "In today's society, death is viewed as a failure of the medical profession. It is the enemy, to be fought at all costs. Death is perceived as abnormal and unnatural, so we close our eyes to the eventuality of it. When a physician says it will be difficult to heal you or you can't be healed, when a disease is diagnosed as life-threatening or incurable, as sad and scary as that is, a gift has been given - a gift of time! Dying can be our finest hour or our most terrifying. Regardless, it is our own personal experience and our ultimate challenge. How we deal with this experience is entirely in our hands, not in the hands of the doctors, our family or our friends. This is our experience and we must take control. There are people who live in the past. There are people who live in the future. But few of us live in the present. Having a life-threatening illness takes away our future and glorifies our past. It gives us the opportunity to live in the present - if we will take it."

Lesson Two -There are "many roads to the top of the mountain." This phrase can be used to describe a wide variety of life experiences. For example, when I use my GPS locator to get directions to a new place, it may give me a choice of different routes - the most direct, the one that avoids freeways or the most scenic. I have to select my preference. This phrase, "many roads..." can also apply to our end-of-life chapter. The choices we make for ourselves and for our loved ones are personal and individual. There are few absolutely right or absolutely wrong choices at this stage. But medical and hospice personnel can give counsel and guidance about all end-of-life choices.

Lesson Three - There is a lot in this universe we don't understand and won't in this life. There have been so many unexplained and unexplainable events that have occurred over the years I have done this work that I no longer think in terms of coincidences. There is a term that Carl Jung coined called "synchronicity," meaning events which appear to have no apparent causal relationship yet, are meaningfully related. I often experience synchronicity in my work and no longer am surprised by it. There is an element of synchronicity in many of the stories in the earlier chapters of this book.

What I have learned from these experiences, however, is to hug more, to be grateful for life's experiences - both good and not so good, to live in the present, to find good in every day and to value all that life presents you.

The end is not THE END. It's merely the beginning of a new chapter.

Appendix A

Graceful Passages
First Unitarian Church,
Albuquerque April 15, 2007

DEATH AND OUR ATTITUDE ABOUT IT

When I was first invited to speak today, I asked for some guidance about the subject matter. I was very graciously told that I could speak on anything I wished. And so, having been given that permission, I want to thank all of you for the opportunity to speak about a topic that many of you may be uncomfortable with. I hope in the process to present some information about death and dying in our society, some experiences I have had as a therapeutic musician that demonstrates the power of music and some thoughts that may enable you to reflect on the end stage of life with new insight and awareness. We can make choices and exercise responsibility in this "middle stage of life" while we are able and while we care that will hopefully help create our own graceful passage.

Norman Cousins, editor of the *Saturday Review* and author of the well-known book, *Anatomy of an Illness*, said, "Death is not the enemy, living in constant fear of it is." We all are going to die, that's a given. Death and taxes, as the humorist quips. But our society is in denial about death. We warehouse many of our elders in nursing homes. We are so busy in this "middle stage" of our life that we often times simply don't have time for those who are in their "end stage" of life. If those of us here today live long enough, this end stage of life, this gradual decline and wearing out of body parts is likely to happen to us all. I'd like to share with you a few interesting and disturbing statistics in order to help move us into a way of thinking about the end stage of life which we are all going to encounter if we live long enough.

The life expectancy of people in this country before the 1900's was forty-seven years. The phrase, long-term care, meant two to three generations living in the same house or neighborhood caring for each other. The current life expectancy of people in this country is stretching into the upper 70's to low 80's, depending on which set of statistics you see. Sixty percent of all Americans will require some type of long term care in their lifetime. Currently, the average stay in a nursing home is three years.

Our medical community views death as a failure. We have the technology and will use it, as well as other extraordinary means, to sustain life without necessarily evaluating the issue of quality of life.

A recent article in the *Albuquerque Sunday Journal* was entitled, *As Death Nears, Health Care Costs Soar*. It discussed the fact that our culture does not want to accept death as a part of the natural cycle of life. I'd like to quote several excerpts from the article. "A major reason so much is spent on health care in the United States is that it costs a lot to die here. For example, of Medicare's annual budget, about $100 billion dollars is spent on the beneficiary's last year of life. Like everything else in health policy, the issue has technological, economic and societal dimensions. It is complicated by family dynamics, the culture of medicine and legal questions, and by personal values, systems and religious views. As more than one physician puts it, ours is the only society in the world that seems to regard death as an option, not a certainty." Remember Terri Shiavo? That situation polarized her husband and her parents, politicians and churches. For a brief moment as news headlines, this situation forced many of us consider the consequences of leaving our own death as an option or to put it another way, totally ignoring the reality of the inevitable.

MUSIC AS MEDICINE

When people ask what I do, I tell them that I am a musician. Most of my work at this stage of my life is as a therapeutic musician. I work with hospice patients, most of whom are actively dying. This is a clinical term used to describe a person's last few hours of life as the body shuts down. This statement about my work often times creates a pause, an awkward silence or evokes some rather interesting responses from people such as, "Oh, I could never do that work. It's too depressing" or "How can you do that kind of work? It must be terribly hard." Sometimes, I say nothing because people just do not want to go there. Other times, I respond to this by saying that the work is not at all depressing. When I, as a part of an interdisciplinary hospice team, can help create a graceful passage for a hospice patient, it can be a really beautiful experience. The team members refer to it as a "sacred moment" or a "good death." Truthfully, this is the most important work I have done. Just about everything in the past sixty years of my life has been in preparation for this work, although I have only recently come to realize it.

The music that I play at the bed-side of an actively dying patient is much different from what most of us think of as music. I frequently use a concept called *entrainment*. This is a term that you see as a concept in physics and engineering hydrodynamics, just to mention a few disciplines. Google the term *entrainment* on the Internet and you'll find a great deal more information. But for a very quick, easy-to-understand example as it relates to music, consider if you pat your foot when you hear certain types of music. That's a very simple example of *entrainment*.

When I work with a patient, I rhythmically entrain with their breathing. I match their breathing pattern. In the final hours of life, there are a variety of breathing patterns as people transition, so I physically breathe with the patient for a short while to get a sense of their rhythm. Then, I play that rhythm. About ninety-five percent of the time, the breathing rhythm of the patient will slow down, relax and settle. I see this change within ten to thirty minutes. Don't ask me to explain. I cannot. For lack of explanation, I tell patients' families that we should all have someone playing a harp at our bed-side. Wouldn't that be wonderful!

Let me tell you about Charles, a really dramatic example of the power of therapeutic music. One of our case manager hospice nurses called me to see what I could do with a patient at a nursing home who was actively dying. The nurse's words to me were, "He lived a crappy life and he's dying a crappy death. I've given him all the pain medication I can. See if you can do anything." How's that for putting the fear in a humble musician? I went into Charles' room not knowing what to expect. What I saw was a rather large man thrashing around in bed. Was he hallucinating? Maybe. I'm not medically trained, so I really don't know. The chaplain was quietly talking to him, trying to hold his hand. But Charles was fighting his own demons, totally oblivious to the comfort the chaplain was trying to provide. So I carefully positioned myself out of range of the patient, should he leap out of bed or throw his leg over the side of the bed. I thought to myself, "Okay, the harp is insured. If he comes out of the bed, I drop it and run for the door. My safety is more important." Now these are not the thoughts I generally have when I approach someone who is actively dying, but this case was pretty unusual. I began to play, not really knowing what to expect, if anything. Charles began to settle down almost immediately. Within twenty minutes, he was calm and asleep. I was amazed and so was the chaplain. I continued to play for a couple of hours and finally left when I couldn't play any longer. Charles died about an hour after I left. Don't ask me to explain. I cannot. I only report what I see and experience. At the team meeting a few days later, the chaplain referred to it as a miracle. That's a bit out of my comfort zone.

Another example of therapeutic music of a much different nature involved Stella. Stella was actively dying and her family had gathered in her room. As I worked with her breathing, using the concept of entrainment, she was breathing a perfect pattern which was a waltz rhythm. I couldn't affect it in any way. Finally, after about twenty minutes, I asked one of her daughters if Stella might have been a dancer. The daughter looked at me in amazement and told me that her Mother and Dad had been wonderful ballroom dancers. Well, I said, I think your Mother is waltzing with your Dad right now. I explained to her what I do with the musical rhythm and the patient's breathing. Then, I played the *Tennessee Waltz* to show her how her Mother was breathing. It was really amazing and beautiful.

None of us know what happens after death. None of us will know until we walk that path and begin that journey. But the image that family was left with made me feel so good about this work. A grieving family had a wonderful beautiful image of their Mom and Dad waltzing together again somewhere. Stella passed very soon after that.

THE POWER OF MUSIC

Hearing is the first sense to develop in the womb and the last sense to go when a person dies. I always tell family members not to say anything around their loved one they don't want the person to hear, even if their family member is in a coma and appears unconscious, even if the family member is hard of hearing, because THEY HEAR. We hear at many different levels with our entire bodies, not just our ears. Live music changes the energy in the room and we can sense this energy at a cellular level. This has been researched, proven and documented. From this, you can imagine the power that music can have in a wide range of life situations in addition to the end of life. We experience the power of music daily. I played for the birth of a baby a few years ago. The mother was a hospice nurse that I had worked with and she invited me to be with her at this very special time in what she called her "sacred space." It was an incredible experience for me. I had not been in labor and delivery since my son was born at Presbyterian Hospital thirty-three years ago. And so, at midnight on a cold night in January, three years ago at Presbyterian Hospital, I was in the labor and delivery room with Kathleen, her husband and the mid-wife. There was a fetal monitor on the baby before he was born, so I could hear his heart rhythm and entrain with it. Then, Kathleen would have a contraction and begin to breathe through it. So I would switch over to work with her breathing. I would rhythmically entrain with each of the patterns. When Donald was born, he was a very content, mellow little guy, he didn't even cry, though he was very healthy and very normal. He heard the lullabies and other harp music that I was playing before he made his entrance into this world. My husband surmised that Donald would always love harp music but never really know why. Another experience that demonstrates the power of music involves a patient who had been an instructor at the Santa Fe School for the Deaf. As I went in his room, there were two of his former students visiting him. I introduced myself and briefly explained my work. Both hearing-impaired students communicated with sign language and one of them could read my lips and had some language capability. After much signing between the students, the student with language ability asked me if the other student could put his hands on my harp. I readily agreed, not knowing what would happen. The student placed both hands on the sound board and I began to play. A few minutes later, as I watched him, tears started streaming down his cheeks. He was "hearing" the music in his own way and it touched him in some way that I, as a hearing person, could not imagine. We sat there for quite some time. I was playing, and he, with his hands on the harp, was crying. The power of music!

Several times, I have encountered non-verbal Alzheimer patients who would begin to sing with me as I played old, familiar songs such as *Danny Boy* or *You Are My Sunshine*. After seeing this happen several times, I learned that music is stored in a different part of the brain from speech. When I play for groups of people over the age of fifty, I usually include songs like *Stardust*, *Over the Rainbow* and *I'm In the Mood for Love*. These songs take many of us back to a time in our lives when we were younger, maybe in love, maybe ballroom dancing. There are individual memories for each of us of different times and places in our lives, another illustration of the power of music.

I'd like to share one final example of the power of music which created a situation of healing for a family at their dying father's bed-side. I had played for Willie a few days earlier when his daughter was there. She was his primary caregiver. When I went to see him the second time, Willie's son and daughter-in-law were also there. There seemed to be some family tension, which is not uncommon. After introducing myself and being given permission, I sat in the back of the room and quietly began to play. Very soon, I noticed the son start to cry. Then, his wife also began to cry. Nothing had been said among the family members. Shortly after that, the son, his wife and his sister all moved to the bed-side together. Then, they held hands. After standing like that for a while, they began to pray. I continued to play quietly. I do not know what had created the tension, but I do believe that some kind of healing took place. I would like to think the music facilitated it.

END OF LIFE CHOICES

I have dealt with end of life patients and death on a regular basis over the past five years and this I know. We have choices to make and responsibility to exercise now while we can and while we care. This end of life stage can be a time of tremendous personal, emotional and spiritual growth, a time of personal and family healing and resolving of family issues, a time to value the forethought and planning you have given to this final part of your life's journey. Some issues to think about now are:

* health care directives - these may include a variety of information
* medical treatment that you may or may not want
* what comfort level you desire
* what information you want your loved ones to know or not know
* donation programs-you may decide to opt in or opt out of organ donation, body donation for research, even skeleton donation.

These are all very personal choices and individual decisions that each of us can make now in our "middle stage of life" while we can and while we care. Hopefully we can create a graceful passage marked by emotional and spiritual healing and growth. And, maybe even have someone playing the harp at our bed-side. I would wish that for all of us. © 2007, Donese Mayfield

Appendix B

REPRINTED WITH PERMISSION – ALBUQUERQUE MAGAZINE

"As you get older, you look back and see there are many chapters in life," says Donese Mayfield, 62. Her recent chapter is the one she considers most powerful.

It began on the day she saw a brochure for a folk harp. In the weeks that followed, the image of the harp stayed with her. Suddenly she was meeting people with harps and seeing them everywhere. The day she learned that a renowned harp builder lived in Albuquerque, she knew it was the beginning of something special. She was 42 years old when she took up the folk harp as her preferred instrument, after playing the piano all her life.

The melodic harp plucked a chord in her soul. Mayfield retired from full-time employment to pursue her love of music. She began performing with flutist Bonnie Schmader and she has produced four CDs.

One day she shared her music with a friend in the hospital. The chaplain heard her and asked if she'd play for dying patients. She said "yes" and discovered it was a beautiful experience. She remembers visiting a patient in Intensive Care who was in a coma. The monitors changed as she played and stopped their zigzagging. Music was clearly easing anxiety, bringing comfort and reducing pain.

Mayfield became a certified music practitioner who is now on-call with Ambercare, the largest hospice organization in the state. When a nurse or chaplain calls, Mayfield packs her harp and rushes to the bedside of patients who are at the end of their lives.

Death doesn't scare her, but she has seen fear on the faces of patients and family members. She would like to see therapeutic music widely available. Mayfield offers workshops throughout the state encouraging others to share their musical talents in hospice or nursing home settings.

On one occasion a nurse called her in to play for a patient who, the nurse said, had lived a "crappy life and he was having a crappy death." He was hallucinating and thrashing in his bed. He had already received the maximum amount of pain medication allowed.

"He calmed down as I played," Mayfield says. "His agitation stopped. Eventually he slept. He left this world in peace and the nurse considered it a miracle."

But caring for elders who are ready to die is different than seeing young people struggle to live. When Mayfield was 60 she played her harp for Lila, a 34-year old mom who was losing her battle with leukemia. Lila's ten-year-old daughter sat nearby as Mayfield tried to bring a soothing light into the room.

When Lila died, Mayfield felt compelled to do something concrete in the fight against cancer. At that time her husband, Dave Bailey, was fighting and winning his battle with prostate cancer. She signed up to walk a marathon as a fundraising effort for the Leukemia & Lymphoma Society's (LLS) Team In Training program. The money raised by marathoners goes to research and patient services.

"Dave and I both do the marathons now. If we can do it in our sixties, anyone can. We've raised over $20,000."

Her message to young people is to dream big dreams but live in the moment. "You never know when your time on earth will be over. So be prepared today."

Bibliography

Ambercare Family Guide to Hospice. http://www.ambercare. com/hospice-care.

American Music Therapy Association. http://www.musictherapy. org/about/musictherapy/.

Cotter, Laurence T. *Sermon at a Memorial Service.* September 15, 2007.

Davis, Robert and Betty. *My Journey into Alzheimer's.* Carol Stream, Illinois: Tyndale House Publishers, 1989.

Hammond, Trey. *A Christmas Letter.* Pastor, La Mesa Presbyterian Church. Albuquerque, New Mexico, 2008.

Holmes, Michael. *Crossing the Creek: A Practical Guide to Understanding the Dying Process.* Reserve, New Mexico: Damone-Rose Publishing, 3rd ed., 1998.

Jones, Moyra. *Gentlecare - Changing the Experience of Alzheimer's in a Positive Way.* Vancouver, British Columbia: Hartley and Marks Publishers, 2000.

Karnes, Barbara. *The Final Act of Living.* Depoe Bay, Oregon: Barbara Karnes Books, Inc., 2003.

Leeds, Joshua. *The Power of Sounds: How to be Healthy and Productive Using Music and Sound.* Rochester, Vermont: Healing Arts Press, 2010.

Sacks, Oliver. *Musicophilia: Tales of Music and the Brain.* New York, New York: Knopf Doubleday Publishing, 2008.

Endnotes

i   "Entrainment," *Wikipedia*, accessed March 30, 2015, http://
      en.wikipedia.org/wiki/Entrainment_(biomusicology).

ii   "That's Entrainment," Keep It Simple 2008 by Van
      Morrison, *Wikipedia*, accessed March 30, 2015, http://
      en.wikipedia.org/wiki/That%27s_Entrainment.

iii   Joshua Leeds, *The Power of Sound: How to be Healthy and
      Productive Using Music and Sound* (Rochester, Vermont:
      Healing Arts Press, September 2010), 37.

iv   *American Music Therapy Association*, accessed March 30,
      2015, http://www.musictherapy.org/about/musictherapy/.

v   Oliver Sacks, *Musicophilia: Tales of Music and the Brain* (New
      York, New York: Knopf Doubleday Publishing, 2008).

vi   Michael Holmes, *Crossing the Creek: A Practical Guide to
      Understanding the Dying Process* (Reserve, New Mexico:
      Damone-Rose Publishing, 3rd ed., 1998).

vii   Laurence T. Cotter, *Sermon at a Memorial Service* on
      September 15, 2007.

viii *Ambercare Family Guide to Hospice*, accessed March 30,
      2015, http://www.ambercare.com/hospice-care.

ix   "Hospice Care," *Wikipedia*, accessed March 30, 2015, http://en.wikipedia.org/wiki/Hospice.

x   "Muscle Memory," *Wikipedia*, accessed March 30, 2015, http://en.wikipedia.org/wiki/Muscle_memory.

xi   Excerpted from http://hospicedoctor.blogspot.com/2011/02/dying-alone.html

xii   Rod Stewart, *Forever Young*, accessed July 2015, http://www.songlyrics.com/rod-stewart/forever-young-lyrics/

xiii Trey Hammond, *A Christmas Letter*, Pastor of La Mesa Presbyterian Church (Albuquerque, New Mexico, 2008).

xiv   Excerpted from http://alzheimers.about.com/od/typesofdementia/a/Whats-The-Difference-Between-Alzheimers-And-Lewy-Body-Dementia.htm

xv   Robert Davis, Betty Davis, *My Journey into Alzheimer's* (Carol Stream, Illinois: Tyndale House Publishers, 1989).

xvi   Ibid.

xvii Ibid.

xviii Moyra Jones, *Gentlecare: Changing the Experience of Alzheimer's in a Positive Way* (Vancouver British Columbia: Hartley and Marks Publishers, 2000).

Made in the USA
San Bernardino,
CA